first you have to say goodbye

A gentle guide for the unfolding self

FLORENCE THUM

Copyright © 2025 Florence Thum

All rights reserved. No part of this book may be reproduced by any mechanical, photographic, or electronic process, or in the form of a phonographic recording, nor may it be stored in a retrieval system, transmitted, or otherwise be copied for public or private use—other than for 'fair use' as brief quotations embodied in articles and reviews without prior written permission of the publisher.

The author of this book does not dispense medical advice nor prescribe the use of any technique as a form of treatment for physical, mental or medical problems without the advice of a physician, either directly or indirectly. The intent of the author is only to offer information of a general nature to help you in your quest for mental fitness and good health. In the event you use any of the information in this book for yourself, the author and the publisher assume no responsibility for your actions.

Published in Australia by Esse Publishing

Printed in Australia

First Edition

National Library of Australia Cataloguing-in-Publication entry available for this title at nla.gov.au

ISBN: 978-1-7642077-9-9

Cover and Interior Design: Kelly Exeter

For Euan and Sian who showed me
ways of being ... my mirrors.

EPIGRAPH

All lives bear traces of the universal.

CONTENTS

A lens into the future	8
The good girl	12
As a woman should	17
Is this?	18
Waking up to myself	19
Lost	21
Mocking words	28
I felt it first	30
New terrains	34
While I was busy	36
Today is one of those days	39
A walk	42
Awareness	**45**
To make a fool of me	48
Human	52
Nerd	54
Sometimes	56
Stop	58
Know	60
Revived	61
Water like words	62
Acceptance	**63**
Am I …?	66
We are done	68
It is time	72
Beauty undeniable	75
Reality	78
Accept	79

Openness & willingness	**80**
I wait	84
To my younger self	87
All is said and done	89
Alone	91
Compassion & kindness	**92**
Let me hold your hand	95
Tortured soul	99
Kintsugi	102
Today	106
Forgiveness	**107**
Isn't it time?	111
Memories	114
Those moments	119
I choose	120
Solitude	**121**
A return	122
This dark night	124
Today I practise	126
Dear One	129
Standing	132
A final word	**133**
Acknowledgements	**135**
About the author	**137**

A lens into the future

THIS BOOK was sparked by the dissolution of a 20-year marriage and a desire to understand what happened.

It's not a story of a marriage gone sour. It's an exploration of the power we have to change how we've been conditioned to approach our relationships with ourselves and others to forge a different life. It reflects a journey of self-realisation that took many years and has fuelled an expansive future.

That journey revealed the shared experiences and common humanity that binds us all. It exposed me to the healing that can come from the writing process and the surprises that can come from examining our lives.

In reading this book, I hope you will hear your voice calling out to you and see perspectives that inspire you to reconsider.

To begin a new life—a different life—we must be open to the possibility of change. We must have the courage to say goodbye to those things that no longer reflect or serve us, a past that is both beautiful and hurtful. And the openness to embrace the new.

For so long, I had eschewed poetry and rejected it as too sentimental and superfluous to my highly rational, functional and accomplished life.

Yet, it was poetry that catalysed my journey of self-discovery and growth. It was poetry that awoke me from the slumber of ignorance and habitual blindness. It was poetry that sustained me through the liminal period of forging a new life.

I came across 'The Invitation', a poem by Oriah Mountain Dreamer, during the first year of my firstborn's life.

I was 30 at the time and as I remember it, it was the constraints of motherhood and the diminished identity of a professional woman that brought me to the poem. I remember it shining a light into my soul through a breach in my 'ordinary' life. It knocked on the door to the self I had put away—hidden, ignored, shamed into oblivion. Its light awakened a longing for my truths, whatever they might be. It caught me straight between the eyes—I had nowhere to hide. And for the first time, I did not want to.

It provoked me to take a closer look at myself; its seductive questions invoked a curiosity about my capabilities and who I truly was.

But awareness is not action. Answering the invitation would come later.

Life as I knew it continued on the outside. But the light of this awareness shone into more and more darkened spaces within. The knock intensified over time.

Fast forward a decade or so, and I came to a pivotal period in my life. Heading towards midlife at the time, many would label it a midlife crisis. My discontent with my family-focused life was at boiling point, and I was once again thrust into rediscovering the self I had been while living a functional life that tied me to familiarity and complacency. I doubted myself and feared the worst.

This was when 'Love after Love' by Derek Walcott found me.

The vision of me, standing before a mirror and loving who was reflected: the person I sensed deep within, beyond the shadow I'd become, a person wholly and authentically herself … this became my inspiration, my raison d'être.

This time, I could not turn my back, so I began a five-year journey of self-discovery.

It was during this time that the poems in this book emerged. They are echoes of the life I ultimately said goodbye to, the journey of letting go and what it took to forge a different life. They are the 'sounds of my heart' (心声).

The words in these poems are feelings and impressions. They are reflections of my personal reality at the time of writing. They are not universal 'truths' nor intended to be 'weaponised'. They are how I sought to make sense of what

I'd gone through in order to forge a way forward.

Ultimately, I learnt to love myself, be grateful for who and what I am, and be enough.

I am proud to say that today, in answer to this: *I want to know if you can be alone with yourself and if you truly like the company you keep in the empty moments*, I can say 'Yes'.

But first I had to say goodbye …

The good girl

I WAS BORN into a Chinese family in Malaysia. My parents were loving and strict and prioritised education. My upbringing was conservative and Christian.

My gender was a culturally perceived flaw I compensated for by being more 'like a boy': highly rational and intelligent. My mother's desire for a 'real daughter', whom she could go shopping or cook with did not materialise. There were some moments, but only a few. My mother's identity was role-based, as mine would eventually become.

So, I stepped into my father's shoes: a world of books, studies and constant striving. I stayed there for my entire childhood and into my early twenties. I remember a happy childhood, purposeful and filled with activities. The importance of continuing to advance in whatever I did was instilled in me. Progress was measured by effort and productivity. More was always preferred. Success was achievable as long as I was prepared to face any challenge head-on, persevere and never give up.

I cannot say I was sleepwalking through my entire life to this point. My life had a purpose: being the best academically.

My dedication and single-mindedness saw me achieve excellent grades, recognition and accolades. I was an accomplished young lady, having also learnt to play the piano and paint. Whatever little time was left for leisure was spent in healthy pursuits, namely exercise, for it, too, served a purpose.

There were also the gendered responsibilities and duties of the eldest daughter. From early on, I was taught to be responsible: for my family's honour, my mother's feelings, my father's pride, my brother's wellbeing and behaviour, and my academic success. These expectations accompanied me throughout my life.

It was important to me to succeed in whatever I set out to do so I could be worthy of my parents' love and care. My achievements were never allowed to get to my head. My culture dictated children and young people were to be seen and not heard, that who you were would be reflected in your actions and not words, and that community acknowledgement of one's success took precedence as a measure of worth. As a daughter, being quiet-spoken, caring and docile was also expected.

The status of being a 'scholar' in a Chinese family cannot be underestimated. To meet my unwavering goal to excel academically, I was prepared to pay any price (though I did not consider them sacrifices at the time). I did not attend parties and had few friends, so focused was I on being effortful and intent on my studies. Youthful fantasies of teenage romances and daring adventures of exploring different lands were lived within my sanctuary of books and music. Books were and remain my friends.

Throughout my youth, I cultivated a persona of someone strong and silent, serious and intelligent, capable and determined. Ironically, in my teenage years, this gave me a voice louder than the other women and children in my family and thus, a certain freedom. I could speak up and be heard. I could draw boundaries that had long been overrun. Such is the prestige and privilege of academic achievement.

My persona as an 'intelligent thinker' was enough justification for creating my own space wherever I was, for being uncommunicative as I withdrew from the noise of familial and societal expectations. I retreated to my room whenever I wanted, contrary to cultural dictates which demanded respectful presence.

I'm grateful for these circumstances of my childhood and teenage years, which allowed me to cultivate a rich internal life. But externally, I played the role expected of me. I was intelligent and had lots to say, yet I stayed silent. I was curious and wanted to try new and different things, but I stayed inside the lines, docile and obedient. Any 'rebellion' occurred in the internal world I created for myself. Unconventional ideas swirled in my mind, but anything subversive was done in a 'nice girl' way.

Despite being female, I was the shining light of my family, the apple of my father's eye—a role model in our small community. I was loved, wanting for little, and assured of my place in that world. Deep down, I longed for the life of a free, liberal single woman. But in my cocoon, I was content to be the good girl, the conscientious scholar. I was the envy of many for being my parents' own brand of adored 'princess'. Perhaps my desire to study abroad was my bid for freedom from the scrutiny and stricture of that life. And perhaps so was the marriage I embarked upon. I did not know this then.

Unsurprisingly, the good girl went on to become the good wife. I met my husband at university where we were both studying law. It was an 'opposites attract' scenario—I was structured and a planner, and he was not. I was introverted and reserved, and he was not. So we got married. We lived busy professional lives and very different 'outside of work' lives. I loved being at home. He preferred to be out partying. Any qualms I had about our differences were squashed by my lifelong conditioning that I could make anything work if I worked hard enough at it. Ten years and two kids later, I was still working hard at it.

Looking back, I recall anxiety and dread as being constant companions throughout those years. It felt like I had a sword perpetually hanging over my head. I was only as good and successful as others would acknowledge me, and there was a constant fear that I would one day lose the love, regard and respect of others. External validation is insidious, especially when it becomes the measure of your enoughness. Questions such as, 'Am I productive enough?' or 'Have I done enough?' plagued me.

These questions, unfettered, eventually became 'Am I good enough?' Every criticism and every denial I received in my marriage suggested that I wasn't. And these thoughts continued to swirl in my mind, in the empty moments of respite from the busyness of my midlife.

Subsequently, I resigned myself from getting what I desired. In hindsight, it is frightening to see how, over time, we learn to make do emotionally, how we learn to downplay and set aside our needs and desires, our dreams, and how we begin to expect less.

As a woman should

Nothing left to say
in this weary grey world
Ploughing on
as a woman should
Her thoughts, who can see?
Her mind, who will appreciate?
Her heart …
her heart, who will hold?
The words forming
The number running through
Her presence a norm
Hardly noticed but
always missed
But for what, she may ask
Her mind, her heart?
What is it to be?
Never you mind
She will carry on
As a woman should.

Is this?

Perhaps I am after all destined

To a life of plans and rules

Perhaps I am after all merely

Denying this inevitable truth

Perhaps I have dreamt enough

And time to return to the ordinary life

A man who loves me

Children who respect me

A job that pays the bills

A few holidays thrown in

What more should a woman ask?

Truly.

Waking up to myself

IT WAS THE late 2000s, and I'd relocated from urban life to the country. To the external observer, it looked like I had escaped the rat race, and life was idyllic. As a new business owner, I had the flexibility to spend time with my children. I had my family around me and a home large enough to meet everyone's needs.

In reality, though, I no longer understood what I was capable of or where I was heading. The nagging sense of worthlessness that had been background noise in my life for so many years started to become very loud.

This was when 'Love after Love' by Derek Walcott found me, with a longing encapsulated within.

'The time will come
when, with elation
you will greet yourself arriving
at your own door, in your own mirror
and each will smile at the other's welcome ...'

While recognising this and articulating it to myself felt like an essential first step, it's hard to override your conditioning. My adaptability, ingrained in childhood and enhanced by time spent as a foreign student and then a migrant, meant I overcompensated for the uncertainty and insecurities by continuing to be busy and active, 'in control' and organised.

I was covering up for the fact that inside, I was lost and aimless.

Lost

Lost

The flurry of activities

The juggling of tasks

The clamour of people

The distraction of noise.

Lost

The connection that matters

The invitation to embrace

The peace of solitude

The centre of being.

If only …

IT TAKES TIME to wake up and become aware of our surroundings and place in the present moment. In the midnight hours, we may dream of our wishes and hopes or fears and uncertainties. But it remains dark. The only respite comes in moments of oblivion—where sleep keeps us from the possibility of hopes or fears and numbs us to feeling anything except the stupor and elusive security of slumber.

In the light of day, there is no time to think as we engage in the doingness of life.

I'd created a busy and high-achieving life. I was a lawyer, a mother, a wife and a daughter, 24 hours a day, every day. I was also a something-in-law, sister and aunty. I performed each of these roles with great aplomb, guided by centuries of traditions and decades of social expectations.

There were fun times. And, of course, it felt rewarding to be a 'successful, responsible adult' doing 'the right thing'.

All these factors make it easy to stay asleep, ignorant of the possibility of a different life. There is such warmth and security in the familiar: an immaculate home, organised days no matter how busy, and established routines with few surprises. Children added to the compulsion to remain in control and not veer from the known path.

As a child, I had big dreams—of dispensing justice and saving the underprivileged. I dreamt of having the authority and power to do good, of having a voice that was heard and respected. This led to a career in law. A curious and serious child, I was single-minded and determined to achieve my dreams. Yet, I was also taught not to rock the boat from a young age. The consequences of doing so were clear. Women who did not conform were labelled 'mad', 'bad' or 'sad'. As a teenager, I recall being admonished for daring to suggest an alternative viewpoint to an uncle during a family gathering, and the look of disapproval shot my way. And at my mother for her failure to teach and discipline her daughter.

Therefore, I learnt to tread carefully and gently, soothe rather than anger or disappoint. Most significantly, I learnt to put aside my displeasure and dissatisfaction and make the best of my lot in life. My 'lot' was rewarded with many privileges, ironically disentitling me from voicing anything that could be deemed ungrateful, disloyal or unbecoming of a lady. An unobtrusive retreat to my room was often the best option.

I suppose a time-honoured career in law was right for me, where within the tradition of the legal profession I met those dreams.

Back in my adult life, by most measures, I had a fine life. But I was a woman who long denied her voice and had unconsciously hidden herself. This was something deeply felt, though not yet identified. What I didn't know then but know now is that it was the emotional load I carried that troubled me.

I remember feeling resentful at having to come up with the perfect Christmas gifts each year for everyone—both sets of family. This included the shopping for and wrapping of all the gifts. No assistance was offered because I was doing such an excellent job of it. Any irritation on my part was seen as an indication of a lack of generosity (so I was told). I can still tap into the clawing guilt that followed and the feeling of being a not 'good enough' woman.

Having a perceived 'good life' came at a price. It was silencing. When things did not go as planned, guilt and shame assailed me. And this motivated me to strive for betterment because that's what I was conditioned to do.

The saying 'ignorance is bliss' is true in our human experience. The wilful or inadvertent denial of our painful existence allows us to function and persevere despite the wounds in our lives.

So we stay asleep. But we cannot avoid dreaming. And we cannot avoid the nightmares—each like the other, repeating in an endless loop until we choose to confront them or are forced to.

Beyond the dark night of sleep, we go through our day in a foggy state—doing what we ought to, meeting the expectations we have long been accustomed to. We no longer question the busyness of living a 'normal life'. The damaging relationships and hurtful conversations no longer surprise us.

Approaching my 40th birthday, I ran away from home. I went on a month-long solo travel stint—something I had not done for over a decade. It was a distraction from feeling deeply unhappy within my marriage and dissatisfaction with my professional life. The compromises I had made in both my personal and professional lives accentuated the not-good-enough feelings. It was therefore exhilarating to recapture my agency, independence and autonomy.

And then, in France, I had my first panic attack. Being somewhere beyond my sphere of control and the sense of 'freedom' were almost too much to bear. Thankfully, the rediscovery of pleasure—the solitude, freedom to think, feel and do when and where I wanted to—was a lifeline. It was something I will not forget and has continued to inspire me.

But then, of course, I returned to 'normal' life: functional, irreproachable, responsible and ongoingly unhappy in my marriage. I sought to influence what I felt to be necessary and positive changes. The message I heard in response was that I was the one who was too conservative, unadventurous, serious and unfriendly. My personality did not gel with the Australian culture of laidbackness, imbibing alcohol, and being sporty and extroverted. I was 'wrong', and my behaviour was unacceptable.

Over time, the hurtful words penetrated the confident facade and lodged in place. I believed what was told to me and of me. Voicing my opinions led to me being accused of being faithless, pessimistic, unappreciative and critical.

These words of Oriah, from her poem 'The Invitation' reminded me,

> 'It doesn't interest me if the story you are telling me is true. I want to know if you can disappoint another to be true to yourself. If you can bear the accusation of betrayal and not betray your own soul. If you can be faithless and therefore trustworthy.'

(At this point, I need to acknowledge that any conversation or argument is a dialogue of at least two points of view, informed by oceans of personal values, beliefs and perceptions from a vast terrain of defences. No one is wholly 'correct'. There is no absolute 'truth' even though each participant in the conversation thinks there is.)

Despite seamlessly falling back into the habits and conditioning of the life I'd created, France had unlocked something in me. There was movement inside, my inner voice recalling that private space in France and beckoning for change. So, I began a course studying the human condition. I did not then know the impact this would have on my life.

This was followed by a tentative step to exercise my voice. I started blogging as an act of courage—to test whether I was creative and could write. Initially, I hid behind an anonymous profile. This allowed me to keep going when I doubted myself, wanted to be hypercritical of my writing and questioned the utility of what I did. With my identity shrouded in mystery, I gave voice to my fears, thoughts and questions to the world. I was fortunate to find a supportive blogging community.

Blogging was a band-aid for the discontent of my work and the duties I carried out each day. It was an attempt to carve out time for me, as were the walks I took in the morning. As I committed to giving voice to the thoughts and ideas swirling in my head, I enthusiastically shared my blog posts as a way of sharing me, my thoughts and feelings. Repeatedly, I heard my ex-husband's discontent and censure for spending too much time doing something 'unproductive' and that what I wrote was superfluous and inconsequential, unlikely to gather a large audience. His failure to recognise that this was more a creative expression of my thoughts and feelings than anything else was disturbing and disappointing. The lack of interest in and behind my writing was hurtful.

Mocking words

A tired mind
A weary heart
Bereft of words
Immobilised.

Stranded in space
Alone, forlorn
Mocking words sound
Piercing the brittle soul.

Shards of glass
Rains, punctures
Prisms of colours
Shielding its nature.

THE WORDS THAT denied my experiences and feelings cut deep. More severe fractures continued to appear. When promises were perpetually broken, I was the one who was too harsh calling them out. I was too serious and to just 'enjoy myself' when I suggested leaving a party before drunkenness and insolence set in. All the way along, I believed that despite our differences, we had strongly shared values. The incongruence between his words and actions made me question *myself*, seeking to be better, to make things better.

An introvert with few confidants, I felt trapped within the illusion I had created of the good life—a successful career, a gregarious, witty husband, beautiful children and the modern version of white picket fences. The loneliness was palpable while I continued to distract myself with blogging. There were few I could speak with of the ills, flaws and cracks in my marriage.

As my confidence in myself and my place in the world waned, I grew weary, brittle and sensitive. The heavier the weariness, the sharper his words cut. Finally, I became too weary to maintain the facade of nonchalance, too tired to find excuses for his behaviour, and too ashamed to keep lying to myself.

I felt it first

I felt it first
A sigh, it drifted my way
Without pause
Unexplained cause

I heard it too
But I did not listen
Consumed by a love
Sweet romance

I knew the moments
The space in between
Words spoken, unattended
Yes, I felt them there

I saw in wary eyes
An expression of doom
Indulgent but not really
A certain malaise

I felt it then saw
A clearing of rose-tint
The stark reality
The woman that I am

I sensed a dis-ease
No more the beguiled
No word to cajole
No place to hide

I sensed a reticence
Disenchanted, disdain
Of the doing and being
No longer entreat

What shall it be
When the hammer falls
To break this fragile
Facade of a life

THE SIGH THAT did not make a sound, yet heard for the first time, came after years of resignation. The arrogance that I alone brought this about so I alone could fix it fell away. I heard the sigh when I could no longer hide from this light peering into the many cracks when it became unbearable.

Our conversations were peppered by heavy silence—me holding back from voicing a concern, from expressing a contrary view lest it would be considered pessimistic, critical or unsupportive. I dreaded gatherings. I no longer enjoyed celebratory events as a bad turn inevitably followed them. Many happy occasions became messy nights of arguments. A business venture went sour with devastating financial impact. Timeouts became the justification for obsessive behaviour.

My life became an emotional rollercoaster, but years of conditioned responses caused me to wonder (briefly even as I write this) if I could have been less 'demanding', more compromising and understanding.

I withheld to keep the peace, as many of us have done so throughout our lives. (And not just in personal relationships.) It's always worth stopping and asking yourself how being silenced, not speaking out and maintaining the status quo serves you.

The sigh, reminiscent of my mother's sighs through her decades-long marriage, was frightening. It foretold a life I had no desire to fulfil.

I recall looking at myself in the bathroom mirror one morning and seeing slumped shoulders and red and puffy eyes. I remember trying to psych myself up for the day. And in that moment, another vision crossed my mind of the young girl full of confidence, with an indomitable spirit and drive to succeed. Where did she go? Who was this person in the mirror, resigned to living this life? This life, which, to external and material assessment, was the envy of many, which others worked towards. Did I have the right to want more?

I continued to live in false hope, believing the apologies and the promises that often came after a downward spiral. I continued to tell myself these were the normal ups and downs of life, and I ought to be able to deal with them.

All the while, I waited like a wound-up spring for something that would give me sufficient reason to justify leaving this life I'd created. Not quite understanding it had to come from within me. Do I love myself enough to demand a better life, a life worthy of me?

New terrains

it says my choice
reflects 18
yes, there are days
I am 18 travelling on
in dreams and hopes
fantasies without a care
without the weight of life and living,
until a jolt of the track
brings me back to present
of a life half-lived
full of promise, responsibility
of unfolding and becoming;
emerging
sometimes limping
occasional skipping still
moving forward hoping this train
will cross new terrains
to sights not yet seen.

WITH OUR history deeply ingrained and one I was unaware of, I looked to the future with trembling uneasiness. I directed this nervous energy to build the limiting future perceived by my blinkered sight. With eyes only ever focused at the distance, we cease to appreciate what is right before us. We fail to appreciate and be truly open with our senses. How could I not see the signs, messages and beauty of the present?

To be present in our subconscious and conscious minds each day seems impossible—plain hard work. Being present to the thoughts that flood our minds and the emotions that surge through our body, requires a steadfastness that comes with commitment and practice. Do not shy away from the pain that may surface or the joy arising; be prepared for them all no matter what and trust that you have the capacity to bear them all. But these were lessons I had yet to learn.

While I was busy

While I was busy making plans
though not unaware
it slipped from my grip
should not have hung on so tight
it was never to be so
the lightness of togetherness
lost souls of that moment
clinging to lifebuoys
till the storm passes;
now look on grateful
waves have calmed
we pass on the high seas
hands raise in recognition
familiar smiles comforting
to know we had been
restoring faith once lost
knowing we may never be
so let go watch it float
where to yet unknown.

AT THE SUGGESTION of my therapist—who now resides in my heart as the wise woman I seek out, whose voice I hear in my confusion—I committed to writing down my dreams as soon as possible and preferably in my state of semi-awakeness. Her feeling is that it should be recorded if it's strong enough to alert you to its presence. And so I did. Like free writing, there was no time or space for editing and analysis, instead, it recorded what was in my mind as the images, thoughts and words flowed.

One vivid dream has me standing at the end of a long pier, waiting for my ride to arrive. I had run to the edge in a long, flowy dress—an outfit I rarely wore in real life—and in true romantic sense, the wind was blowing through my hair. A jet ski came by at great speed. I somehow managed to hop on as a passenger, and we left the pier. I was swiftly taken to a large boat where a private gathering seemed to be happening. Climbing the rope onto the deck, I felt excitement, curiosity, and a sense of being entirely at home. A mysterious presence led me to a long table occupied by a group of men. I sensed a familiarity and recognised two elders from my family. What transpired was a conversation in which I staked my place at the table and spoke with a voice that was loud, clear and feminine. The next scene took me to the prow of the boat. I entered a boudoir with satin sheets and sheer curtains surrounding a four-poster bed. On the bed was the most majestic tiger with whom I felt such ease. I could hear the sounds of waves as the boat's bow slashed through the ocean. I could feel the wind billowing through the curtains. A sense of freedom and peace engulfed me.

This was a snippet of the same dream which came to me at different times during this period. The symbols and signs were clear. I was leaving safety and embracing the feminine within me. The tiger was a symbol of strength, power and courage.

This and other dreams gave me access to an unseen self. The self I knew, intellectually and consciously, was a construct of my beliefs, conditioning and interactions with others. The dreams opened up dialogues with which I felt compelled to engage. In these conversations, there was no right or wrong, good or bad, but rather a consideration of 'how' and 'why'.

Were there other ways of being 'me', a woman nearing midlife? Were there different ways of being in this world? If I wasn't concerned about what others thought or believed of me, would I behave or do differently? What was beyond the conventional life I led? Was there such a thing as 'normal', and if so, what characterised it? What was this dissatisfaction, this disgruntled, resentful sense bubbling to the surface?

So many questions. So many welling emotions.

When we notice unpleasant emotions, it's instinctive to push them aside or minimise them as the effects of daily stresses. But we ought not. Every emotion has an origin— fear or love. Moving through our emotions helps us to move on.

Today is one of those days

Today is one of those days
The rain does not soothe
The grey cloud oppresses
Today is another of those days.

The spirit cannot soar
The soul in aching lack
What is to become
Of this dim vision, dark and gloomy.

Yes, a call to surrender
To let, let it all go
To not heed the laughter
To not care what may hurt, to destroy.

Impossible to rise
Above the crashing waves
Sinking, fighting afloat
There is no compass pointing home.

Today is one of those days
Though rare, it must appear
Shattered dreams always lure
This melancholic mind reaching out.

Smile, it will be better
Smile so no one sees this
Smile so your mind can be fooled
Smile, none may solve this crazed puzzle.

Pretending merrily
The calm serenity
It too shall pass, it's said
This complex facade, never fear.

Today is one of those days
Just one, of those days
Of marked indifference
Holding on to the flicker of light.

IT WAS THE morning after another night of interrupted sleep. I was accustomed to the 'big night out on the town' pattern now: the first phone call signalling the long night ahead and the final phone call requiring me to leave home in the middle of the night. The worry in between would put me on edge and make me anxious and resentful. There would be anger at myself for the continued facade of 'nothing is wrong'—the pacifying, scolding and moderation to minimise any disruption to a sleeping household. Tending to him out of duty—because it was the 'right' thing to do. My pride driving me to hide and brush over the cracks in my marriage, pretending indifference the morning after.

I saw the illness, but I had no control over it. I had run out of solutions—none of my interventions succeeded. So, resignation was where I landed. I got on with it as a strong, capable woman ought to. Duty bound.

Despair and anger—at myself, my life and others—assailed me. These lows were managed with self-soothing gestures: hobbies, rigid control of my environment, and a focus on perfection. All were signs of avoidance and a refusal to interrogate my emotions.

Each day, I lifted myself and did what needed to be done. Being conscious of this was a rare glimpse of my capacity and this was enough to give me a certain self-assurance to evaluate my life so I did not abandon my soul.

Why am I here? What do I have to learn?

A walk

I took a walk today
Searching for a newness of breath
To caress my weary soul
Watching clouds roll by
Wishing its lightness would somehow
Reassure the promise of time,
And the trees of silver and green
I saw dancing without care
Their promise a new day will dawn.

SO I TOOK morning walks. For anyone who knew me well, this was so out of character. But they were the one thing that allowed me to escape my life, to claim whatever I could of myself and my space.

Music accompanied me—music I could not play at home for fear of being mocked for sentimentality and lack of appreciation for 'real music'.

These walks were like balm to my days and nights and the hope for a new dawn each day. They were a lifebuoy for days spent drowning in the many tasks of being the lawyer, the manager, the emotional support person, the fixer, the motivator and the carer.

The work I had done to get to this point—to care enough for myself to take this time out began many years ago when I had cultivated a mindset to examine my life. During these morning walks, I also found clarity, at last, an emotional language to describe what I was going through. Some of the poems in this book are a product of this.

In 2015 came the straw that broke the camel's back—the point of no return.

It was my birthday and a working day. By lunchtime, he said he'd done enough work and was off to play golf. I was disappointed he chose that over the opportunity to spend the afternoon together. But he proudly told me he'd organised for my mother to prepare a birthday dinner for me, and we'd be having this with the kids and our parents later. I spent the rest of the afternoon working, and he came home an hour later than the appointed time for dinner. This was a familiar occurrence for us who waited, and when confronted with a less than warm reception by us all, he was indignant. I was offered an 'apology', swiftly followed by a remark that I was being too sensitive and ungrateful.

There are no doubt many sides to this particular story. And in the end, it's not about who was right or wrong. In any relationship, personal or professional, we can only listen to ourselves—to the feelings and experiences as they build over time. If something feels 'wrong', if there is ongoing discomfort, unease and distress, it must be acknowledged.

The causes of this sense of wrongness require exploration and examination—not to blame but to understand and work through.

In that one little event, I experienced a lack of empathy, care, connection and intimacy. I felt unheard, unseen, belittled. It told me that, indeed, the relationship had been over a long time ago, and I had held on out of habit, the 'good girl' conditioning, and fear of an unknown future should I let go.

In the end, I had to ask myself two critical questions.

What do I value more—a self I would respect or the facade of a happy family for the world to see?

What do I fear more—the obliteration of the me that was still hidden within or being on my own with a family to care for?

Ultimately, I chose me because I knew that effort brings results and that I would survive the emotional upheaval, the physical displacement and the disrupted family life. Most importantly, I knew I could better care for my family by being wholly present to myself.

Awareness

SOMETIMES, we hang on too tightly and for too long. We hold on to what we know because of what we've invested and what we hope will eventuate.

A common barrier to resolving disputes is a party's obsession with 'sunk costs'. This is the notion that because one has put in so much effort or expended so much time and money, it would be unimaginable to accept anything less than the sum of these costs plus some more. There is no backing away. Quitting is unimaginable.

Stuck in this mindset, we continue to invest more time, effort and money. In the context of relationships, it is even harder to divest from what is a significant emotional investment. Add to this the stigma in having a 'failed' relationship; growing up, we are taught that fickleness is a flaw and virtue is shown through persevering, persistence and never giving up. Leaving a relationship seems like a loss in a win-lose situation and is a significant knock on our pride.

So I spent the most time defending and fixing in the 'sunk costs' headspace, too stubborn and too proud to admit 'defeat'. Whenever there was a setback, such as when the relationship was highly volatile, when a business venture failed, or when a career faltered, I went about setting it 'right'. The more difficult the circumstances were, the harder I worked to make up the losses and fill the gap. Covering up and camouflaging was what I did best.

I spent years sleepwalking. Each disappointment, each setback, was interpreted as building endurance. To admit failure was to tacitly admit to the negative choices I'd made that had piled up—the decisions I'd made that were destructive to my sense of self, the opportunities my fearful self did not take.

Eventually, the time and space for awareness arrived, and the sensation that things could and should be different became overwhelming. The danger here is allowing that sensation to grow into a compulsion to do 'something, anything'. Because doing 'something, anything' could be similarly destructive—not only to us but also to the people around us.

I had to resolve to consciously do 'something, not just anything'. And that took me on a path of growth. I opened up to examining my life, to new knowledge and experiences beyond the usual, and to doing familiar things through different approaches. I stopped with the avoidance and running away.

To make a fool of me

Running

Forever running

From what, do you know?

Yes, but I can't, I won't

allow it

To touch me

When did I become so cynical?

When did I stop believing?

I will not go there

To the place of dreams

To believe its existence

For its demise

Would be a death knell

To my soul.

I say this best

Expect nothing, live in the present

Am I still scared?

But I'm still running

To this heart of mine

I have mended

In order to be free.

Well can I be,

Free and beloved

Isn't it selfish?

This faithless self

To see another's tears

The joy, the euphoria

They cannot last, or can they?

I desire, I resist

I laugh, I cry

What is this thing called Love

To make a fool of me.

WOMEN HAVE long been touted as the nurturer and the carer—the glue of the social construct known as 'family'. Part of this construct dictates that it is socially acceptable for a woman to be aggressive in protecting her children; after all, it is in the interest of another. However, a woman aggressively protecting her professional turf and fighting for equality is often a cause for censure. A woman looking after herself and her own interests is still perceived with wariness.

I was privileged to have the mental space to consider and reject some of these stereotypes. Yet it still took years before I could honestly confront how they played out in my life. The narratives of supportive wife, devoted and sacrificial mother and 'superwoman' are unattainable goals, but I still tried to achieve them anyway. It took the rumblings of dissatisfaction to grow incessantly loud before I could admit my life had to change or I would be totally suffocated, that I would become physically unwell.

Knowing your life has to change is one thing. The 'how' is another.

Having always been an avid reader, books became the rock ledge holding me sufficiently to peer across the other side. The chasm remained dark and dangerous, filled with lies I had told myself, the stories I had created to quiet the rumblings of the pain and fear permeating my life.

But when the rumblings worsened and threatened to unsettle, I had to understand why. I had a seemingly good life, so I was supposed to be content. A woman ought not to be greedy to want it all or to prioritise something other than what society and culture dictate to be her lot in life. Or can she?

I was drawn to studies of the human condition. After all, how could I see if I only sat looking in and sometimes with one eye closed? Turning around and looking within with eyes wide open were prerequisites to my studies. This purpose gave me courage, and a different world emerged.

Human

A busy mind
A productive day
A structured life
A familiar default
Or a conscious act.

Guilt and shame
A sense of wrong
A need to justify
A reason to assure
Or merely to ground.

Not knowing, lack
A tremor in comfort
A dent to confidence
An image of small
Or a human response.

ENROLLING IN A postgraduate degree in psychotherapy came down to finding distraction from my problems, in something valuable and of deep interest to me. Each one of us will have our own 'study' or ways to deepen awareness of ourselves and our life beyond. The 'reason' I gave to myself (and everyone) was that I would do something wholly mine for the first time in a long time to indulge in an intellectual interest. In reality, it was so much more.

I found frameworks, perspectives and philosophies, and more importantly, a whole other approach to what it means to live and how to experience my world. I had to dig deep to arrive there, excavating the long-buried desires, forgotten dreams, entrenched beliefs and assumptions. I had to remove layers of conditioning, deception and artifice, one layer at a time. I had to move from a highly critical, polarised, fixed view of right and wrong to see the grey in life. I became aware of other perspectives and able to see the world from another's lens. It extended beyond the development of the intellect to an existential exploration.

We have unique avenues to explore what makes us wholly ourselves—what sparks joy, what lifts us, what our values are, what we are willing to put up with (or not), and how we can live authentically. For me, it was through the portal of curiosity and learning.

Nerd

I read so much
Can't remember the details
Only shapes of letters
Imprinted in my mind

Love is transient
Taken for granted
Man is inherently selfish
I the only given

There will be lessons
In perpetual repeat
Until they are learnt
Until it is done

Until I am no more
A speck in the wind
A glow of sunlight
Floating in eternal bliss.

SO, WHAT WAS I to do with this emerging awareness?

It would have been easy to retreat. I could distract myself, forget this path I had stepped onto, and retrace my steps to the straight and narrow. And it did happen—temporary returns to the 'old ways', buoyed by temporary okayness: a holiday, a new challenge, some diverted focus. But once our eyes are open, we can't unsee.

The happy outing with friends begins with a lunch stop where the alcohol flows and then doesn't stop for the entire weekend except for when we are asleep. The concert in a beautiful vineyard degenerates into an embarrassing encounter with other concertgoers. Many supposed-to-be intimate couple times deteriorating into caretaking duties on my part.

Shame, anger and resentment collided in a ball of fury in the face of these things. Masking my feelings with outward nonchalance and emotional withdrawal were my coping mechanisms.

But I could not continue to do it. I saw the fear in my life and knew turning back would be in its service. Something within me—the potential death of who I am—said, 'no more'.

I suspected venturing into unknown territory would bring uncertainty and potential suffering. But the intensified rumblings refused to be ignored.

Sometimes

Sometimes
We fail to pay attention
Fail to perceive the changes
Fail to see the ones we love

Sometimes
We fail to rein in
The thoughts in our minds
The images in our eyes

Sometimes
We fail to recognise
The life we have missed
The ones we love and lost

It is then we notice
What we have left
The remnant of a life
Too late to regain.

THIS TIME, it was my children who were the catalyst. I would discover years later that they had experienced an anxious, highly strung, teary mother who faked a smile or two. They knew when their distracted mother wasn't listening. They knew when their mother was unhappy and distressed.

I was forced to confront the example I was setting for my children: settling, putting up with and enduring, denying my passion and direction, accepting self-imposed mediocrity. What journey would I inspire in them with this example?

So, in the name of love, I acknowledged my flaws, delusions and less-than-stellar performance. I threw myself into my studies, taking every opportunity to explore my human condition. For the first time, I intentionally chose to step out of my comfort zone, to befriend and trust the therapeutic processes and the people I had around me. I opened myself to change, for change to find me.

As the Oscar Wilde quote goes, 'We are all in the gutter, but some of us are looking at the stars …'. That was indeed my internal life. Looking up, I saw another life, a different life—which might not prove to be better, but at least it would be one I chose consciously, mindfully, and with my eyes wide open. Perhaps this different life was just 'not this life'.

With this awareness, I chose to be present and open to the possibilities my life might hold.

Stop

Stop

Enough of your doing

Lay down your pen, your ladle, your device

Lay down the capturing, the producing, the finishing

Lay down the 'what-if', the '5 minutes more', and 'I'll be there'

Breathe and listen

To the sounds of life and living

That you take for granted

The sounds which come and leave

In a heartbeat and never will be again

Breathe and watch

The faces that watch you

smile and your tears welling

The faces that encompass the living and the dead

The dreams and hopes of lifetimes

Breathe and feel

within you, all that surge

for attention and the love that comes in many forms

Desires which you have in not attending

left to wither and pass

Stop.

Enough of your doing.

Breathe.

Know

Whatever they say

You know who you are, and more

Know your name, my dear.

Revived

You have eluded me for a thousand years
A million steps taken in your presence
I feel you, your whispers haunting me
Taunting, mocking of this life
I reach out never grasping
The essence of you, I hope
Would guide my return, alive.

Water like words

Water cascading
Like words on a page
Reminder of past hurts
Etched into my skin
Watching it bleed
Washing away.

Water cascading
Like words on a screen
Bringing renewal, healing balm
To a soul seeking
Rest now, my child
All is well.

Acceptance

MARRIAGE IS THE commitment to maintaining a relationship with another. Within this commitment, I believed trust and loyalty to be critical factors. Despite my trust being continually broken over many years, my loyalty to the person and the social construct remained—loyalty I expressed by excusing his actions towards me and others and minimising my emotionality in context. Perhaps it was also my approach of treating marriage as a project I did not want to fail. All this saw me stay in the marriage well beyond its use-by date.

Early in my marriage, at a time when I needed solace and was desperate for a solution, I picked out a book about surrender. I recall a strong resistance to the central theme of the book. 'No, I will not surrender. My life will be as

I perceived it, decided it, and envisioned it to be. I am a highly intelligent, capable woman, and if there is a problem, I can and will fix it; I will find a way.' That's what I told myself. Surrendering seemed like 'giving up' at the time. It was the antithesis of what I perceived life ought to be. Yet the struggle was real. The internal conflict between what a wife was 'supposed' to do (be supportive of her spouse and work to overcome tribulations together) and what living in a way that was authentically me persisted.

The codependent nature of the relationship made my 'sacrifice' logical and sensible. Marriage, after all, is forever, is it not? So I put aside my desires and ignored the deep sense of dis-ease, that something was not right for me. This even after I had tried different methods of reconciliation: changing him, changing me, changing our environment. Nothing worked. It takes two to tango, and it often felt like we were dancing with different partners.

It would be easy to look back at my choices at each turn and judge them as 'mistakes'. Choices that purportedly kept me safe, secure and comfortable, but ultimately, stuck. But that would be unfair to me and the ones around me. I did not get to where I am today without the tribulations of those days past.

I accept that at each moment in time, we make the choices for which we are best equipped, emotionally and psychologically. The interpretation of the events leading to that decision and the consequence or outcome anticipated are simply the stories we tell ourselves. We lie to ourselves so our lives seem palatable. Work was indeed stressful. We were coping the best we could. I chose to believe the behaviours that upset me were 'a necessary evil' and acceptable for networking purposes. It took me a long time to admit that I was complicit in creating that life. This is not blame or guilt, but rather a realisation. In my desire to protect, through a sense of duty, I took on managing, changing and indulging; to keep fixing what was broken, to fill the emotional gaps and to put up as a woman should.

I kept feeling there was more for me in this life than what I was experiencing while berating myself to be grateful for all the good things I had. When intellectualisation failed to provide an answer, I moved to the practice of mindfulness to find a decision point. What I found was more than I had hoped.

I was introduced to mindfulness in my therapy training. On one hand, I was dismissive of its potentiality; on the other, I sought relief from thoughts running amok in my mind. The latter required me to trust that letting things be and letting go of perpetual fixing could possibly be a solution. I had to accept some things were beyond my control. I learnt equanimity.

Am I …?

Am I to tell myself
It will be okay
Sorrow is to be expected
But hey, what's life without a bit thrown in?

Am I to say to all
Who would listen
I don't mind because I know
I understand the truth within the lie?

Am I to smile
An attempt to assure
I can sit with uncertainty
Experience my teacher, haven't I been there?

Am I to comfort me
When the night is cold
A lesson will present itself
Healer, teacher, a life of learning?

BEING CONTENT is a state of mind, of finding peace with the material world. Frankly, I didn't need more. I had the house, holidays, clothes, cars and the like. I was beyond survival in Abraham Maslow's hierarchy of needs. I was grateful for the material things and the people that gathered around me.

Gratitude is more than being grateful or gratefulness. Gratitude is an awareness of all that has shaped us and an acceptance of its many effects without regret. The adventures, the hurts, the love, the rejection, the disappointments—everything that's made us who we are.

When I asked, 'Is this enough?' I wasn't asking about what I had materially. The question becomes: Are we, each of us, enough to ourselves? Do you like you? Do you recognise yourself?

The rumblings I heard on the way to letting go were the knocking on the door of the cage I had created to meet the expectations of the world. The knock asking whether I was living the full expression of myself. Was I being true to me? Could I leave this cage in order to find my home?

This is subjective. To be true to myself, I chose to love without compromising my integrity. I chose to express myself as I saw fit without harming others. I chose to inhabit my space unapologetically.

And all these things I accepted for myself, no longer denying their value or validity in my life. I accepted that changes would have to be made.

I accepted that I had chosen the straight and narrow path, which kept me secure but also clipped my wings. I accepted that change was necessary.

We are done

I don't want your adoration
Only your care
Words here and there
Of 'how are you'
'Thinking of you'
And 'miss you so'.

I don't need your protection
Only your concern
Words across the sky
Of 'will you be safe'
'Are you alright'
And 'take care of yourself'.

I don't need your declarations
Only quiet gestures
Words signifying
'I remember'
'I'm with you always'
And 'I will see you soon'.

Alas, we are done.

YET DOUBTS assailed me. The status quo is challenging to discard. Tied to it was a world of status and identity—the safety of familiarity. Knowing change is necessary is insufficient to preclude the fear and trepidation of what would be. The safety of the familiar keeps its firm hold.

Do we need to ensure a soft landing before we step off? Are we aiming too high or for too much? Are we worthy of that which we dream? Is it just that? A dream, a fantasy, a fairy tale? Should we be more realistic?

Perhaps desperate times called for desperate measures. The constant rumblings were too much to bear. My attempts to stifle the noise had been temporary fixes. Professional achievements, solo travel and playing at domestic bliss hyperfocused on parenting, kept me busy and ultimately drowned out the noise. But it remained, and each time the busyness stopped, the noise intruded, each time louder than before. The continuous shutting down was exhausting.

In the wake of yet another conflict, I returned to the concept of surrender. This time, I chose to surrender, or so I thought. What I had actually decided on was resignation—to accept my lot in life, to put up with what I sensed was not right. I did this for the right reasons. And the truth is, I did not listen to the inner knowing that said 'wake up'. Energetically, this is the polar opposite of the acceptance that would come later.

Must we always pull a face resembling a smile when all we want to do is rage? Should we lower our expectations in order to live amicably? Can we live contentedly by choosing to avert our eyes and hearts from what displeases or distresses us? What proportion of our life must be 'alright' for that life to be 'worthwhile'?

I accepted that, with few exceptions, any and every family outing would involve me driving home and taking care of the children and often looking after a husband who had too much to drink. I accepted that my job was to arrange and organise all family events—birthdays, Christmases and anniversaries. I accepted that it would be ungrateful or ungracious of me to expect assistance, to request help, and to expect this work to be shared because I was 'privileged' to be flexible in my work schedule. I accepted the narrative that as a mother, I was privileged to spend time with my children and to look after them, while being a full-time professional working flexible hours. I accepted that, as a woman, I ought not to question bearing the emotional load in the relationship.

The 'surrender' I practised was a taken-for-granted, do-not-complain, compliant type of existence.

I consoled myself by saying everyone has difficulties, so I had no right to complain. I was not worthy, so I minimised 'I' and 'me' to escape or avoid the mental anguish and emotional conflict I was in. My privileged life was like a death knell to me because 'other people have it worse'. 'Knowing my place' was another inheritance from my childhood and normative culture.

So, it is not in everyday motions that we choose to leave things be. Instead, it is a state of mind that says I have to see and acknowledge everything that is happening—to come out from behind the rose-tinted glasses, stop acting under my superwoman persona, and accept that I cannot fix this and leave it be. This was a bitter pill, an identity crisis for someone who has long been a 'fixer'. Being the 'fixer' was so much a part of me I had even made it my career. As a lawyer, problem-solving is the most essential skill. My career reinforced that sense of being in control, not showing weakness and ploughing to the ultimate goal.

I'd been conditioned to believe the ability to come up with ideas and solutions would make me 'visible' and elicit affection. To step away from this path, set since childhood, meant relinquishing an identity and the emotional and mental security that came with it.

It is time

Drained, bone weary
Consumed and spat out
There is little to the reserves
And I suspect it's all my doing.

The world continues
On its axis, spinning
While I circle my life
In confusion and despair.

Yes, it is time
To let go, to let them go
To where they belong in their world
While I salvage mine.

Let sanity return
Love and a certain peace
For none will be as precious
As the terrain in my mind.

AS I RETREATED to my sanctuary of books—first to escape, then to intellectual rationalisation and finally to solitude and reflection—I traversed the long and turbulent road of becoming someone I would respect.

Going off the well-trodden path sometimes allows us to experience a new view and see different sights. Sometimes, it is even safer. I was bushwalking one day, and being an inexperienced walker, I followed the well-worn path of many who had gone before me. It seemed the sensible thing to do. Before me I saw the path ahead which required me climbing over a large boulder. I hesitated. Off to the side was a narrow flat ledge but muddy. I had a choice to make. For me, there was a real possibility of slipping as I climbed the boulder; I chose to step off the well-trodden path to the side onto muddy soil. Doggedly following the set path could be treacherous indeed.

Going off the set path was a decision only I could make. Not so much from bravery but rather necessity born of a desperation to prevent a spiritual death. We can't wait for the path to clear before we take a scary step. We take the step despite the fear, and as our steps grow, we realise our courage in the hesitation and the persistence of each step.

I started engaging with interests I had put aside for years—writing as I wanted to, listening to music I liked, saying yes to experiences I would not have entertained before I questioned the status quo.

I did not step off to escape. I stepped off, not knowing the outcome, with no assurance of what the future would be. From the many near financial disasters I had salvaged, I realised my capabilities and learnt to trust myself. I was adamant that who I am is enough, that who I am means I will survive yet again, and this time on my own terms. And so I accepted all the possible consequences of this action I would take and the responsibilities that come with it for the people in my care.

The decision to leave a 20-year marriage did not come easy. The marital relationship was a knitted ball of thread, some threads woven tightly, others less so, ever so complex. On the eve of the monumental separation, which came at the end of an emotionally difficult six months, I was a full-time parent of two adolescents with only part-time work, and supporting my parents. I had to trust in the promise of a brighter future. I had to be mentally and emotionally prepared for financial insecurity. I had to commit to being the emotional and psychological safety nets to the ones who needed me most.

Despite the stressful time, there was an undeniable sense of rightness—the hope that the future would hold more than just surviving. I refused to leave this world with regrets because I did not at least try.

Beauty undeniable

Throng of people
Passing by
From my bubble, I watch

Private lives
Common experiences
Unique expressions

Joy, love and triumphs
Despair, fear, disappointments
Never the same

Throng of people
Passing by
Beauty undeniable.

ACCEPTANCE certainly isn't passive, nor is it comforting. There is peace in accepting the past will remain in the past. There is peace in acceptance in the present. However, the future is still a scary place for those who are planners and prefer certainty.

I spent years searching for me, fossicking the parts of me I had so cleverly buried. The parts I hid in shame and ignored to survive in the world in which I found myself, oblivious to the masks I had put on and the adaptive behaviours I adopted in the restrictive world I had chosen to live in. Watching how I had chosen these without consciously knowing I did; I was indeed sleepwalking. By not making a conscious choice, I had chosen nevertheless.

Having accepted the past and the present, the questions remained: What to make of the future? How do I make the right choice? What, indeed, is the right choice?

Engrossed in the cycle of anticipating, planning, making and revising, we look to an outcome we can only imagine in the present. We lose our vision. We struggle with the right choice, and so we put off, avoid and get anxious over it. So often, we fail to listen to ourselves—to that which calls us, to that which puts a smile on our faces and usually, to that which makes our hearts beat just a little faster. So often, we limit our world and options because we are too afraid to look outside this world.

Acceptance that I have little control over the future leads me to this. The only choice is the one we make now, in the mindful space of what we believe, know and feel in each moment. The future is the response; the outcome will unfold without our control or intervention when we tend to the present.

I have long since believed, intellectually, that I am a speck of dust in the grand scheme of this existence. I am stardust; we all are. I have also now accepted there is no 'Me' in the grand scheme of life. The identity of 'Me' is created at the intersection of our relationships and our choices. 'Me' evolves every moment and through every choice we make in those wakeful moments. Our identity is created in the choices and decisions we make. For the first time in a long time, I am tenderly excited about who I might become.

I am accepting that while I am powerful in my life, in my potential to contribute to the greater whole of this existence, and yet I am so miniscule is humbling. It compels me to look beyond what is me and my world to others and beyond. And this would eventually open a door for me to re-engage with my dream of serving justice and the underprivileged, this time through a healing process.

Reality

Your beautiful promises
I've heard them often
Filled me with hope
Like this, do not become reality

I can't, I won't wait forever
There's no reason to explain
For if my hope brings us pain
Then it's best I leave, our story done

On your tear-streaked face
I can't see your truth
So let me say this one last time
A heartfelt 'I love you'.

Accept

Whatever unfolds

However it unfolds

I accept

I am grateful.

Openness & willingness

ONE THING about acceptance is we do not get to pick what we accept and deny or reject. What is, is. The true essence of acceptance is to embrace the whole of life, of us as people in our world, our history. Only then can we stand on higher ground and look across the entire terrain of this land we call our life with clarity.

When I reached this point, I could see the well-trodden and covered paths not yet traversed. I could see myself more clearly—who I was and what I became. Most importantly, I saw the becoming versions of me. There was sad recognition of the times I did not make the 'right' choices, where I avoided the emotionality and rationality of the past and was scared to stand up for my values and who I was, where I capitulated and enabled. The story I told myself back then was that I was 'just adapting'. And there were consolation prizes that made up for the pain and retreat into oblivion.

Inoculated against the pain of disconnection from myself (and others) and surviving in a state of slumber, I recognised I was doing the best I could at the time. I know now that we must be ready to wake up and take action before change can happen. It cannot be forced. Getting ready took me many years. Time is relative, and being ready to change will take the time that is needed. Ultimately, this is an exercise of gaining the self-awareness and motivation to change your life.

I see a past filled with imposed narratives, cultured expectations and societal norms, few of which I questioned. Those I did question and engaged in an activism mindset with, I then promptly relinquished in the name of 'peace and harmony' and family. The struggle to like the person reflected in the mirror was deep. Looking back, I see a woman who did not love herself, and now I know why. I was ashamed of who I was in my adopted land, who I had become, who I allowed myself to be, and the life of resignation and camouflage I was living. The pain intensified when I stopped respecting myself, and my integrity shattered. I was far from who I was, who I thought my self to be, the identity which held me up; I no longer recognised myself.

Humans need to feel connected, to belong to a community. This is our survival instinct. I recall being alone in a foreign country, my sense of self-preservation, protection and survival activated. Refusing to be defeated by the isolation, I set out to find my place. This place could only include me if I conformed to and performed what was expected of me, denying the personal expressions of cultural and familial beliefs and values. An intelligent person, I read the signs well and adapted quickly, not just in public but also in my private life. Over time, these adaptations became my default behaviours. I stopped questioning and reflecting on who I had become, what I had given up and what I had gained.

Language is an imperfect but necessary communication tool. Labels are limiting, yet they carry a nuance and convey a common understanding. So how did a 'strong woman', a declared feminist, end up being a 'doormat'?

The answer is fear. For a long time, I feared opening my eyes to the realities of my life, both pleasant and unpleasant, and the opportunities that would bring. I was fearful I would not like what I saw and critically, not be able or good enough to change it. Over time, I realised I was limiting myself and not recognising my inherent resourcefulness. I became open and willing to see the pain. But that meant I was also able to see the love I had around me, and the strength and resilience that is within me.

I have always been a curious person, the child with lots of 'whys' from her lips. So when I began my psychotherapy studies, it was for both a long-held interest in the human condition, and a deep desire to understand the emotional struggle I was experiencing. In the intellectual sense, I was open and willing to learn. I recall the first classes involved learning the skills of person-centred counselling and being required to role-play. I had the choice to superficially attempt these exercises, or fully engage with the process. The fears came back. That vulnerability would be perceived as weakness. That I would be exposed as a person who did not live true to her values. For my problems to be found out as small stuff or unimportant. That I was unimportant and my stories were the fiction of an overactive imagination.

Within the learning environment, familiar and thus safe, I took a gamble. I opened myself to others, and most importantly opened myself to me. I resolved to face up to myself, my circumstances and the excuses I made in and for my life. I decided not to prejudge the outcomes and instead went with the flow of the learning. I worked on learning one day at a time, living one day at a time, choosing to be amazed by the discoveries and new insights. I resolved to make positive changes no matter how difficult or confronting or unconventional. I resolved to be patient, and to take steps as they presented themselves. I learnt to trust the process of self-discovery and growth.

I wait

A fist clenched around my heart
A storm swirling in my mind
What am I doing
The pain I am causing

The distance between us
The connection so tenuous
The shifting sands of time
An eternity, a wink of an eye

The future seems so hazy
I am lost and half-crazy
For this was not my intention
Yet here I am with full attention

How will this eventualise
Will this dream be realised
Oh my intellect is silent
And my emotions resilient

I wait.

WHEN WE ARE lost, it's important not to react, but to stand still, take stock, formulate a plan so we can find ourselves again. Listen. Observe. For me, solitude became a friend, sometimes the only friend. And into the empty silence, I poured myself. Being with pain is not an overstatement, it is necessary. The ability to be with your pain is learnet … and it is always with a knowing, a trust that the relief and light will come. I had help, a wise woman who gently pushed me and supported me to look at the darkness, to acknowledge the fear and also the courage and strength within.

And so the process of taking a hard look at myself began.

I saw flaws, some of my own doing, some not … nevertheless all mine. My mindless reactions and decisions, my reactive coping which hurt and disempowered, my cowardice in the guise of surrender. In my tight hold on my marriage, I might also have denied another the power of choice. In my attempts to fix and restore, I might have refused another their agency and growth.

Along the way, I also learnt the difference between feeling sorry for myself ('It's my fault'), feeling victimised ('It's your fault'), defining myself in my stuckness to a current reality ('I am powerless', 'I can't'), and the honest appraisal for growth.

It was not pleasant in the least to encounter the less shiny parts of me, the fragments in various aspects of my life where I'd unwittingly hurt others, and the moments in which I could have lingered a little longer or shortened, the people I failed to stay connected to and those I let in for far too long. None of these were fatal to the life I'd forged, but they were all flaws I had to reconcile.

Despite a certain sorrow attached to the realisation that we are flawed, we can choose to look to the future instead of feeling sorry for ourselves where we are. We can choose to focus on making positive changes. We can choose what to do so similar mistakes are not repeated.

One thing we are tempted to do and sometimes succumb to, is to blame others for our mistakes. Perhaps this is our attempt to exonerate ourselves or to see the best of ourselves.

'If *only* so-and-so didn't do that, I wouldn't have …'

'*What else* can I do but …'

'*Of course* I must defend/protect …'

These are all familiar phrases, similar to the child-like school-yard exclamation of 'they started it …'. But we are not victims, passively being acted upon. Rather, we have the potential to be active agents to be better versions of ourselves.

To my younger self

Perhaps I'm a fool
Perhaps I know not what I need
Why can't I just let it be?
Isn't this life enough?

For I can't bear to look at the reflection
And see one I don't respect
One who has given up, resigned
Seduced by circumstances
Lacking spirit, vitality
Never living the passion
I so deeply feel within
And so this is why,

Perhaps I will regret
Perhaps I never did understand it
But I know I'm on my way
On my way home.

So take my hand, my sweet
And walk this road with me
For every rock underfoot
Every shower overhead
For chilled and weary limbs
I know I've got you to lighten the load
A friend who listens and understands
Who will love me nevertheless.

WE HAVE OTHER options in how we respond to and in any circumstances. We can choose to make a different choice; we just have to be aware of the moment of choice and decide to take responsibility for our response. Perhaps 'even though so-and-so did that, I will …' 'I choose to …' 'If I must defend/protect then I …' can be alternative phrases in our self-talk.

The paths taken or not taken, divergent from my values confronted me—the things I let slide because it was easier to let them be. Perhaps if I'd been less scared, more courageous, and taken action for change sooner, I might have prevented loved ones from being exposed to distressing experiences that have left deep wounds. In my sense of powerlessness, I did not see the alternatives and options that were present. I couldn't have known whether these divergent paths would have led to better outcomes in parallel lives. I accept I will never know the outcomes of the 'what-ifs'—the present beckons.

All is said and done

When all is said and done
I am only flying home.
Like the young curlew flying
Not knowing, north
Assured only by collective memories
Of a past not lived,
Universal in nature, instinctive.
Carried on the wings of others
Gone before, in trust
Of the flock marshalling its strength
Never ceasing its formation,
Forever holding, eternal love.
When all is said and done
Love, me, myself and I.

KNOWING THAT every moment brings forth many options is enough of a lesson. There will always be imperfections in how I live my life. And this was the lesson I carried with me as I approached the moments and decisions at this time.

Awakening to the reality of my life and being conscious of all that had passed hit me hard. Yet somewhere deep within, an echo sounded. It says *I am better than this*. It says *This will not define me*. My children's faces imprinted on my mind's eye, their expectations, my hopes. Here is the light that still shines within.

In our darkest nights, when we cannot see the way ahead, when we operate with anxious energy, agitated and confused, when we believe we have no answer, we settle into what is happening. We open ourselves to possibilities we had not previously considered and become willing to take the offers we had shied from. We head towards the glimmer of light.

This journey took time to happen. Each step took a conscious effort and a willing heart. All the while meeting the daily demands of life.

Alone

Being alone is an art
A choice at times
And perhaps not

To be complete in oneself
With the thoughts that swirl
Of love and despair
Of care and neglect
Of intent and ignorance
Of power and helplessness
Of trust and disbelief
Of faith and doubt
Of living and dying
Of being and doing
Of trying and allowing
Of receiving and giving
Of happiness and hurt
Of acceptance and anger

Being alone is an art
Of gratitude and grace
Of ultimate love.

Compassion & kindness

I AM ONLY human, I told myself. It's an acknowledgement, not an excuse. It was a hard sell to begin with because being human means being okay with imperfections, being flawed at least some of the time. But like any habit, time and practice paid off.

I resolved to be less demanding of myself, less harsh on my flaws and failings, and more compassionate. I began to refute the fearful voices that shouted 'not enough', voices that told me I ought to expend greater effort, to find better solutions and greater achievements constantly.

Whenever a problem arose, I was quick off the starting block to resolve it. Family and friends came to me for solutions, or so I believed, and I gladly obliged because doing and resolving reinforced my sense of worth. It patched up the world of 'not enough' within, but only temporarily. Once one is on the rollercoaster, it's not easy to get off. There is a high to appearing stronger, more intelligent and more capable than others. Like a drug, we need more of it each time to feel the same high. I solved perceived problems when often, what was really required of me was to listen. I had applied the same diligence to various aspects of my life including marriage and parenting, exhausting though it might have been.

We must learn to be aware and recognise when the 'not enough' voices are making critical judgements and demanding their 'shoulds'. When we can recognise those voices for what they are, we have space to choose what to do with them. These voices may sound like:

'Work harder, you're so lazy.'

'You need this to look attractive.'

'I'm not qualified to do this.'

'Life is leisure, stop pressuring yourself.'

What voices do you hear?

I set out to change these internalised voices by firstly understanding what drove them and then facing the fears they engendered. Mindfulness practice helped me stay focused on the present, learning to stay with my fears. I learnt not to react and 'make things good' each time a problem, real or perceived, arose.

To those loud voices, I learnt to say, 'be gone'. They had served me well and perhaps they would again. But for now, I needed to listen to the tired and desperate voice within—

to let some things go, to let some things be, to leave certain things where they were.

When my rational mind had run out of excuses and justifications, when my soul was weary from rejecting its calling, when my spirit was battered from the failed attempts to take flight, I had little choice but to extend compassion to myself as I had to others. I learned to be kind to myself.

Let me hold your hand

My child, let me hold your hand
Let me sit beside you
I can see the pain etched on your face
I do

I know it's hard
I know you are trying to be strong
My sweet child
The courage you show is admirable

But I know deep within
You are afraid
I can't promise soon all will be well
But I know you will be stronger for this
Yes, you can't see how

But in time
Soon you will look back
And see this moment for what it is
Grace
You will be a woman you can be proud of

The tears gliding down your face
Shows a heart that's breaking
Also a heart that loves and cares
A heart that feels deeply, yearns for much

Your passion will guide you
Just let it be, my child
And let us just be here
In the dark silence

My child
Rest your head on my shoulder
Let the tension go from your being
Just for a little while
Breathe deep
Know that I love you.

FOR EVERY VOICE I recognised and called out, there were perhaps many more that I didn't. The point is not to do it all but to know we are on the journey. For every voice we say no to, that is one less to be burdened by.

Being mindful of each moment becomes a habit. A smile alights my face for each triumphant choice not to listen to these damaging voices.

There is an energetic difference between the voice of 'not good enough' and 'I can do better'. If you close your eyes, take a few deep breaths and listen, the voice that lifts you, opens you to possibilities, expands your chest and breathes easy, that is the voice you follow. Not the one that makes you shrink or hide, which makes you cower inside, which makes you constricted. That 'not good enough' voice can sometimes masquerade as one that seems to 'make sense' or one that feels comfortable.

On this path, I also practise compassion and kindness towards others. I was a novice and probably still am. A hard taskmaster to the self is likely a hard taskmaster to others. I might have been conditioned to behave in specific ways for reasons of love, necessity, and tradition and culture. It would have been easy to lay fault at another's feet but my decades-long state of oblivion was my responsibility alone. What I'd gone through was my life lesson. No one knows what I'd be without it, but I know I'm a better person having stepped on this road.

It is always possible to see the better side of another while still wearing the reality lens on one eye. We can entertain alternative meanings in another's words and actions. And we must take responsibility for our interpretation of them. And in our response, evaluate its impact on another. Our response-ability is within our control, and we need to exercise it with compassion and kindness.

This does not mean the outcome will always be rosy. I had to remind myself I'm not responsible for how others interpret my words or actions, nor am I responsible for how they choose to react. That responsibility lies with them.

Extending kindness and compassion to myself took time and particular attention. It is harder than being kind and compassionate towards another.

Tortured soul

In that moment of clarity
I see the grace of God
In that moment of love
I see the Universe conspires
To bring light and hope
To a tortured soul.

A soul longing to be free
A brilliant mind wanting to take flight
A human calling out for salvation
And traversing this long road
Will all be put to right
At our journey's end?

IT WAS SUMMER. On school break, my children and their cousins had been stuck at home while their parents worked. Knowing how much they wished to spend time with each other I organised a late afternoon swim at a local waterhole.

I left work early and took the daily 90-minute commute home. As I neared home, I rang both sets of kids in their homes to get ready, with instructions on what to pack. After a quick change of clothes and with my children in tow, I collected their cousins and we spent summer dusk at the waterhole. While they played, I pulled out my laptop and resumed working to make up for the early departure. To top this day off, I prepared a home-cooked meal for all as the children were having a swell time and I didn't want to break up their fun.

While I enjoyed seeing the fun and happiness on their faces, I recall being super-tired that day though feeling satisfied for having been a 'good' parent and aunt. In hindsight, a get-together for pizza would have sufficed to satisfy the kids. This is but one instance of many in which l over-extended myself.

I often dismissed my own needs under the guise or self-imposed illusion of what others needed or expected, and in the hope of being good enough in the eyes of others. But I could no longer do so, nor did I wish to do so.

Not every moment is a teaching moment or a learning moment. Not every moment needs to be effortful and purposeful. There were beautiful simple moments if only I was open to them: time to pause, take it easy, listen to what my mind, heart and body needed, and be delighted.

Getting to the place of knowing I have always been good enough took time and effort. This was a place I spent much time reading, exploring and reflecting to arrive at. I gave my attention to concepts, ideas, aesthetics, activities, words and moments which resonated with me.

One word that resonated was 'kintsugi': the Japanese art of repairing broken pottery by mending the areas of breakage with lacquer dusted or mixed with powdered gold. When I embrace the beauty of kintsugi, I see beauty in all things, perfectly imperfect, including the human expressions of love and this human life.

Kintsugi

Like the cup
The zen practice
The shards of glass
Broken and whole

Bound by gold
No attachment
Perfection in flaws
Vulnerable and strong

THE HOPE AND deep-seated belief that 'I'm okay, and things will be okay' emerged. My education, knowledge, experience and skills provided an assurance of my place in a materialistic and professional world. Through the years on this journey, I gained confidence that I could take care of my sanity.

I reimagined what 'okay' meant. I needed to re-examine old standards and expectations, look deep within for my own standards and expectations, shed and embrace, modulate and interrogate many years of lived experience to catch glimpses of who and what I wished to gather as me.

At the time, and perhaps even as I write this, I wasn't sure if it was kindness. Still, I was determined not to pathologise the relationships, demonise the people involved or blame others for my circumstances. Having accepted where I was, I was taking responsibility and ownership for my actions, the steps necessary for positive change. And I would bear the consequences. It wasn't resignation, which involves feelings of helplessness, but rather self-compassion.

With these in mind, I was willing to listen to and be gentle with myself, to let go of decades of internalised irrational expectations and reconstruct a 'new' sense of self and being. Through many periods of solitude, I gifted myself the space to stay with the pain and catch the glimmer of light. And this time, with an appreciation of all the world has to offer, gently and kindly meeting them as they arrived, allowing each become without forcing any outcomes.

I was married to an intelligent man. I could see his brilliant mind's potential and the first steps towards change and betterment. I worked hard to motivate him and to change us—ultimately imposing my wishes and desires upon him. For years I took the lack of will as a character flaw, his stubbornness as an excuse. I have come to accept that there is no change until one has the willingness to change.

I have also come to realise that an unwillingness to change does not make a person inherently 'bad'. There are always obstacles to change, obstacles only that person can remove. All of us have places we resist going into. Same for him.

Most importantly, I realised it was not my job to change another. As a therapist, I facilitate. I walk beside my clients as they do the work. As a woman, I can support but cannot force. I can only be responsible for myself. So I choose that now. I resist the urge to fix my feelings of being 'not good enough' by being everything to everyone.

Similar to the art of kintsugi, it is only when we realise that we are enough, that we are humans with frailties and strengths, that we don't need to create perfection in our life, that we can look beyond and see the light.

I watched how the kids stretched their time, full of activities—physical and mental—all while unapologetically claiming time for themselves. To be 'selfish'—when did that get conditioned out of me? Did it serve me? What was the price and the payoff? Recalibrating is always necessary, as we go through our lives. This work of self-growth is never done. We need to be mindful and aware of when the work is required.

In the process of interrogation, revisioning and reimagining, we are empowered to live our best life.

Compassion and kindness begin with me, within me, for me.

Today

I ... see Beauty today

    In the laughter of children

    In the joy of play

    In the activity of daily living

    In the creative flow of words

    In the idleness of conversations

    In the sensuality of touch

    In the warmth of embrace

    In the confusion of mind

    In the breath of body

    In the comfort of togetherness

    In the simplicity of being

    In the peace of flowing water

    In the majesty of mountains

    In the silence of the night

I ... see Love today.

Forgiveness

WITH COMPASSION and kindness comes forgiveness.

I first encountered the word 'forgiveness' growing up in a family practising the Christian faith. It wasn't until I had to apply it to myself and others that I finally understood what it actually meant and what it takes to practise it. I knew then that the price not to forgive was too high: energy-draining, thought-consuming, emotionally-charged days.

To forgive is to lay down the sword we hold over our own or another's head and the shield we hold between us and them; to acknowledge and accept our own and others' imperfections. I don't need to hang on to the perceived injustices and hurt. In letting them go, I am not condoning them. I am merely seeing the humanity in all of us.

Irish poet John O'Donohue said, 'When you forgive yourself, the inner wounds begin to heal. You come in out of the exile of hurt into the joy of inner belonging.' I began this journey.

To forgive comes first from within, a spirit, an attitude and a commitment to not hold onto the destructive emotions that beset us, to gather the resources within us. To forgive is to accept what is past and turn our energy to the present. Unless we are here, we cannot craft a desired future. It is not to hold grudges or blame others; it is to empathise with them and have compassion for their being and doing.

Life happens, but it is not necessarily directed at us, although we may experience its impacts. Within the maelstrom, I still have the choice to position myself, and I choose to start with love and forgiveness.

I forgave myself for the 'wrong' decisions I had made. I recognised them instead as the best decisions I could have made at the time. Today, I try to make decisions from a place of love. Love for those around me, with the hope that they might finally be given the space to realise their purpose, to make positive changes to their lives. Love for myself to not hold on so tightly, to let go of expectations of that elusive future decided so very long ago, and to have unfettered space to create a future life that is attuned to my values and interests no matter what they materially or physically transpire to be.

It only takes one person, myself, to traverse a different path and change a course that will impact many. So amidst the well-intentioned support and call to arms when my marriage ended, I chose to be that person who did not did not give in to societal norms and expectations of right or wrong, good or bad.

With strong resolve, I navigated through the grey of life, specifically the usual separation discourse. Away from the vengeful heart or seeking vindication or compensation, I chose to take the 'higher ground' to the chagrin and gentle admonishments of many. From the normative paradigm, I was encouraged to see a lawyer (the irony is not lost on me), to fight for what I deserved, to 'make him pay'.

For me, the separation came from a different paradigm. Through soul-searching and personal agency, I chose to stop pursuing what no longer serves me, that would harm or hurt me and those I love. This needed to be translated into action. Walking the talk was difficult; for a former lawyer, the talk of rights and entitlements was tempting though I knew it would be destructive in so many ways and especially to the people in my care.

The practicality of the decision was a collaboration. By this point, it was no longer a reactive expression, it was not a retaliation nor was it vengeful or vindictive. This was purely I-centred from a place of knowing what I needed, am capable of and willing to let go of. I felt empowered to have an amicable ending.

For all these, I forgave myself for the impact this choice had wrought on my dear ones, and I forgave because I understood then that we are all at different points of this journey called life. Through the process, compassion and kindness were ever present. Compassion for the other's feelings and for their humanity. Kindness in my actions as best as I could. Demons exist more often in our minds than in the words and actions of others.

Isn't it time?

Isn't it time to do something

Isn't it time to face the truth

Isn't it time to put a hand up

To acknowledge the past

That led you here to

This moment

Of desolation

Of realisation

To the lives you have influenced

The lives you have infected

The lives you have impacted

By the way you live

The love you have lost

The smiles you no longer receive

The joy you no longer feel

An existence devoid of meaning

Except chasing the next drop

Isn't it time?

TO STAND ON ground built upon my values required a spirit of conciliation. It could not be my ego playing 'I am better than …' or 'I can live better …'. Instead, the discerning factor was this: I chose to change my life, therefore I would make decisions that were true to me.

Things happen for one or more reasons or none. Yet often these things trigger responses from us. In our minds, we perceive things as happening to us. But things can just happen, and we just happen to be caught in it. Rarely are we the focal points of the happenings in others' lives; we may be only bit-players. I know I'm not the focal point of others' efforts and actions. This does not absolve me from the responsibility to lead my own life. But this responsibility can only go to the aspects of my life and my world that I have some influence over and can control. Not everyone or everything is our responsibility.

What I perceive and how I respond to the happenings in my life is within my control. So what is the point of all that has happened in my life, to the road taken and not taken, to the decisions made, unmade and not made?

I looked for the meaning of the years lived. Making sense of them, and most importantly, making meaning of them, became a central theme to my everyday living. And foremost in my mind was the refusal to succumb to the victim narrative, feeling victimised and swept by circumstances. If we perceive ourselves as powerless, then we'll react as if we are powerless and we end up being consumed by those circumstances.

Reconciling the knowledge that I'm a mere player in this vast world in which I have little control and am yet powerful, is indeed difficult. Perhaps a way to approach this is to be empowered in that which is within my control, and to leave the rest. And what I can control is how I respond to any situation. Wisdom lies in knowing the difference.

The lessons we take from the challenges in our lives are unique to each of us. I'm not referring to the 'lessons' that serve to restrict or limit us as we move into the future, those which make us cynical of the world at large and angry at those around us, which make us doubt and fear. I refer to the lessons we learnt that empower us to choose and walk an authentic path that is true to our values without apology. There is grace in our approach and in our steps.

Memories

All the mem'ries
Where have they gone?
Though you may search
They are no longer.

So I now speak
A friend who cares.

How long will you
Continue on
Losing yourself
Hating yourself
Finding yourself
Vicious cycle.

While the world turns
But you don't see.

What you have lost
What you will lose
Perhaps it is then
Shadows reveal
Reality confront
Calling on you.

For none can wake
Your slumbering
Until the hard jolt
Life and love lost.

She is long gone
Away from this
Never bitter
Forever scarred.

Yet I wish you
My friend who loves
Wellness and care
Peace in all things.

I REMEMBER the moment when I first knew there were lessons to be learnt.

I remember my children's faces, eyes darting and worry written across their faces as they looked at me, unsure how they ought to behave. And then their tentative smiling. The incongruent attempts at humour to make light of a scary situation. Their assessing of the emotional temperature and attempts to extract themselves. I'd worked hard to protect them from these incidents but I saw their apprehension. As I went into 'damage-control' mode, I'd imagined the example I was setting for them, as a woman, as a parent, as a spouse and as an individual. And I didn't like what I saw in my mind's eye.

So I began with the questions of how my vision of a good person, a responsible person, an authentic person, and an empowered person would live, and how that would look from their perspectives. This was followed by what actions I needed to take or changes I would have to make in order to fulfil this vision. These were my inspiration.

We need to find out for ourselves what motivates or inspires us to be our better selves. I had begun from a mother's place. And my children became the mirror into which I looked at myself.

I also learnt to be mindful and pay attention. Young and fresh, excited about the life ahead, I had imagined a future and believed that the initial bout of imagining was all I needed to do. I failed to reassess, to reimagine. I did not notice that with each moment—every word and action, every decision and non-decision, every relationship I built or severed—my world was slipping away from my vision, and further from my values. Life cannot be a 'set and forget' event.

In the decades leading up to this epoch of my life, the barriers I identified as preventing me from taking action were, in the end, mere excuses. I could have made a change if I had the conviction and the courage. I could have taken action if I had seen what was happening every day, which turned to years, if I had the necessary tools to examine my life. It took me many years to acquire the tools through personal learning, formal education and my wise therapist. In these, too, I forgave myself.

A mindful life, a connected life is necessary. It is not an option.

I was not alone in my journey to separate. My journey paralleled the ones each of my family went through. They had their own roads to walk, their own trials and tribulations, their own fun and happy forgetfulness.

I saw sadness and confusion in their eyes, the occasional fear of not knowing what had happened and what would happen and then putting on a 'brave' face which covered up hurt, disappointment and fear. I offered them the security of my presence and a degree of certainty—that they would be safe and I would be there for them no matter what. They were apprised of ideas and plans, involved in decision-making, and given the autonomy for self-expression.

The marital separation, conducted under the same roof and relatively amicable, wasn't without its angst-ridden and angry moments. Each of us experienced loss and grief in our own ways and expressed our hurt and sadness differently. I engaged with caretaking and working to maintain some semblance of familiarity for the family. We did what we needed to 'survive' that period. Surrendering to the moment, forgiveness was the path of least resistance, and one which opened up the greatest possibilities.

Those moments

Those moments
When you feel you can't go on
When hopes have disappeared
When dreams have all but shattered
When it seems there is no one here,

Those moments
When the skies seem eternally grey
When tears won't stop flowing
When love is distant, fleeting
When all you want is escape,

Those moments
When your desires remain elusive
When pain cannot be dismissed
When hurt can no longer be hidden
When all you've worked for appears futile,

In those moments
Keep Faith
Forgive
Trust
Love.

I choose

I choose to act not out of fear, but
from love instead
To offer grace in most unexpected places,
I choose to forgive and
seek to understand
To offer compassion and yet still,

To allow you to walk your journey and
hold your own energy
I choose.

Solitude

SOLITUDE presents different feelings to each one of us. Some are drawn to it, as am I. Others resist and many others have not even been in contact with it.

Solitude is a state of being alone that we go through at different stages of our lives. It is necessary from time to time for us to remember our past, reconcile our present, and conceive our becoming.

Solitude is a familiar friend to me. As a young child, I often called on it to find solace and comfort from conflict, disruption and impositions. It is a place I am most comfortable in, at peace. So here I returned, a place where I can be myself to imagine a possible life.

A return

So this is how it feels
The first time
As the ground slowly disappears
It is done;
How many times will this repeat
The wish for many or few?
How many more heartaches will be endured
held by the hope of the next union
How many more unions to be celebrated
before the eventual loss cannot be tolerated;
Now it is clear the true meaning
Of returning home.

A mindful life begins with solitude. To have space and to bring awareness to how I was living my life could only occur when I was alone and undisturbed. The practice of mindfulness, immersing myself in me, was a privilege and a lifeline.

I needed to be alone to find myself, to learn how to be with people without losing myself, on my terms and in ways that nurture me and would not harm others. I consolidated the lessons I'd learnt, the new ways of relating from a place of enough, a certain confidence in who I was.

I was alone in spirit, choosing to withdraw and separate myself in order to observe the flow of time in my relationships and craft a life I would not regret living. I stepped out of my comfort zone so I could explore avenues of connection. This aloneness was a separation from all that keeps us busy in thoughts, aroused in emotions and mindlessly reacting and doing. Withdrawing from the noise of expectations and recriminations was a requirement.

This dark night

Nevermore will I fear
the darkness of the night
I have been there
Though not pleasant, it is not
the beast it's proclaimed to be,
There under the glooming sky
I have heard the call of lost souls
I have seen the fake smile of the I-haves
I have seen the despair of the I-wish
But never have I encountered the call
of true souls living their trueness,
Indebted to the darkened mist
swirling in my mind
for through its hazy cold presence
I locate my warm light,
No trepidation of this dark night
Though I never wish to return

EVEN AS WE evolve, we continue to live and function through the demands of daily lives. I could not escape this. There was no actual cave where I could go into seclusion. I was not physically separated from others for long periods.

Yet I had to honour the sacred part of me that sought aloneness, which refused to be silenced, which was now taking centre stage. If I needed to distance myself from those who loved me for a brief period in my life, then that was a price I paid. I had to learn to love myself first and replenish my soul before returning. The stressed, anxious self—even in physical proximity—did not foster closeness or intimacy in relationships.. Counterintuitively, spending time by myself freed me to have a better connection with my loved ones. My calm and clarity permeated the quality of our interactions.

Along the way, I learnt that as I changed, my interactions with others, and thus my relationship with them, also changed. What would happen when I was no longer 'agreeable'? What would happen when I was no longer 'accepting of everything'? What would happen when I made decisions independently? What would happen when my expectations changed? Instance after instance of changing what was no longer true for me. Over time, I experienced and saw these relationships in a new light. And this magnified the positives and negatives of that life, focused my attention and helped me take the next step and then the next. Through this process, some relationships were forged and others let go.

Each new step makes a new path. Each mindful step makes a conscious journey.

Today I practise

Today I practise silence
Silence of the age-old sage
Silence that rings far and wide
Silence that holds a thousand dreams.

Today I practise patience
Patience of an old soul
Patience that carries many faiths
Patience that embraces its own truths.

Today I practise stillness
Stillness of the prayerful nun
Stillness that transcends worldly knowns
Stillness that reaches deep within.

Today I find calm before unknown.

EMERGING FROM the dream state, I finally caught glimpses of light and shadow, noticing their interplay, and realising there was no 'right time' or 'best time'. There was only 'now'. And there would always be 'now'.

Living a life with grace, forgiveness and compassion was something to aspire to. But it was not easy, because we also needed to live with forgiveness and compassion for ourselves and others. Things would not always go smoothly or 'as planned' or 'as desired'. Sometimes we'd have to pay a toll for this road we embarked upon. Mine was of lost friendships, evolving professional identity and loss of some material comforts.

A new path of solitude gave me space and freedom to choose wisely and to adapt. To decide when and with whom I would spend my time and space. It allowed me to evaluate what was necessary and superfluous, how to navigate and perhaps untangle the ties that bound me.

Virginia Woolf posited that *A Room of One's Own* was a necessary condition for a woman to create works of art. What greater creation is there than life? Solitude was that room for me.

How we manifest and express our solitude has implications for those close to us. It is when real conversations are had instead of mindless chatter, when silence is held instead of awkward avoidance, and when relationships are authentic in their sparseness.

I let go of what I knew, with a preparedness to be without many things, and knowing that finding myself and my raison d'être would fill me immeasurably. I was comforted by this.

The security of no risk or loss means we are stuck. And I did not wish to be stuck doing the same. So I unclenched my hands, prying open the fingers that were gripping onto safety, security and stale expectations. I resolved that I alone would be responsible for the decisions made. I would be answerable and accountable to me.

Fear still attended each decision and every step. Yet a dogged determination resting on the knowledge and insights I gained held the fears at bay, mostly. Learning to capitulate to fear and retreating into the 'safe but stuck' zone was a lesson I had to learn.

I said 'yes' to many professional steps, to experiences and relationships I'd previously shied from, conversations I would not have had, and being vulnerable. Life became more enriching because of them.

And with each step, my fears receded. I experienced sufficient safety and familiarity to change and uncertainty, and the okayness and even some 'successes' of not retreating. It was empowering.

Dear One

Dear One
Look at you!

All grown up and independent
You've crossed that bridge
You knew you could
But you had to be sure.

Well here you are
The woman you knew you always were
Who was masked, sometimes hidden.

Look at you shine
You are on your path
Striding forth, unabashed.

How exciting the possibilities
The occasional fear surpassed
You are doing so fine
You are doing beautiful.

You are doing You!

LETTING GO of fear is a monumental task. So we begin with small steps, letting go of the fear of sipping coffee in a cafe alone, dining alone, travelling alone, being alone, saying the wrong thing, disappointing another, looking silly or aggressive, of being 'too much' or 'not enough'. The little steps we take to confront each little 'demon' in our minds is progress, a step forward.

The first time I noticed that things were alright was some three months after I, with family in tow, had moved into our new home. Driving to work, I had stopped at the traffic lights and noticed myself casually resting my elbow on the car door, which was unlocked. This was significant because in the past I had an almost obsessive act of checking that car doors were indeed locked each time I stopped at the traffic lights. The clicking of buttons to unlock and relock when I sat in the driver's seat was an unconscious act evidencing my emotional state. When I saw my car door was unlocked, it dawned on me—I was no longer feeling unsafe, anxious and fearful.

I felt a certain gladness, a lightness of spirit as I acknowledged how far I'd come.

Letting go also requires us to look deep within and learn not to mind the darkness within. We all have these moments at various times to varying degrees. It is alright to be imperfect. It is okay to be afraid. With awareness, we step through it, whether by spending time 'listening' to our self-talk, journaling or exploring possibilities and remedies. Letting go also requires us to draw on the knowledge, skills, people or plans that give us tangible support as we take courage. These I embraced.

We cannot please everyone, and others will likely judge us. We are all different. We all need to look deep to discover our raison d'être, enabling courage and dispelling fears, or progressing despite our fears, taking the necessary steps one at a time into the future. The judgements of others don't need to land on you, or worse, limit you. Judgements are often not about you. Don't take it personally.

The crucial thing is this: we can only stand tall and be the person we truly are when we embrace the feelings and thoughts that descend upon us when we are alone, when we can let go of the judgements that beset us, when we can forgive ourselves and stop apologising for who we are. This is the journey, and each step takes us closer to standing taller.

All these steps, we have to do on our own in order to be free to make authentic decisions for our future.

Standing

Standing
Looking back
Footprints left of the morning journey
Some pelted by the rain appearing at intervals
And the steady footprints, strong heels pressed into the sand
Holding on even as the waves rolled in
Now but just dents on a smooth shore
And the way ahead seems clear
Blue sky, seagulls on their freedom flight
Rain clouds at certain distance
Nothing like before
A tower of strength, a gathering of joy
Waiting across the line at dusk
Life.

A final word

IF WHAT YOU'VE read in this book has provoked you in some way, then this book has done its job. I did not set out to prescribe answers but rather to prompt questions on the process of letting go and moving on.

After all, as Malcolm Gladwell once said: 'The best kind of self-help is not a prescription for how to improve your life, it's a prompt.'

I will boldly say it's always time to explore the assumptions, norms and preconceptions that have shaped your life.

I'm still on the journey. Only this time, I'm awake, conscious and open to possibilities and choices. There is no telling what this life might still require of me, and there is enormous joy and excitement that accompanies this.

> 'And the point is to live everything. Live the questions now. Perhaps you will then gradually, without noticing it, live along some distant day into the answer.'
> ~ Rainer Maria Rilke, *Letters to a Young Poet*

Acknowledgements

I HAVE TO remind myself that this acknowledgement is about my writing process and the sacred space I have been afforded to deeply engage with this indulgent project.

I have learnt so much from everyone who engaged with my writing when I was blogging on *meaningsandmusings.com*. Your insights and support were invaluable. Thank you.

I would not have believed I was capable of writing poems, and as a way of self-expression and emotional release, if not for Ron, whose personal writings deserve their time in the sun. Your haiku challenges were inspirational. Much gratitude.

I am deeply grateful to Lee and Elise, who read versions of the manuscript. You listened deeply and provided incredibly gentle and honest feedback.

Kelly Exeter, the editing process wasn't so bad after all! Thank you for being patient with me and meeting me where I am. I have learnt much.

Unbeknownst to them, my family, who in their own ways allowed me the time to write. Thank you.

And for Euan and Sian, who inspired me with their love and generosity. Words cannot express my love, especially for welcoming me into your worlds.

About the author

FLORENCE THUM is a psychotherapist, educator, and former lawyer. She is a migrant woman of colour, her life and work shaped by movement across cultures, identities, and ways of being. She writes professionally, her work centres on the human experience of change, loss, and becoming. Writing has long been her way of making sense of the world. First you *have to say goodbye* is her first book.

www.ingramcontent.com/pod-product-compliance
Lightning Source LLC
Chambersburg PA
CBHW061209070526
44583CB00025B/3176